T0353729

AuthorHouse™
1663 Liberty Drive
Bloomington, IN 47403
www.authorhouse.com
Phone: 1 (800) 839-8640

Published by AuthorHouse 8/24/2015

ISBN: 978-1-5049-0191-8 (hc)
ISBN: 978-1-5049-0189-5 (sc)
ISBN: 978-1-5049-0190-1 (e)

Print information available on the last page.

This book is printed on acid-free paper.

authorHOUSE®

Presented To:
_____

By: _____

On: _____

CaoDai: A Faith of Unity
A Parent and Child Book

Hum D. Bui, MD
Hong D. Bui, MD

Edited by Ngasha Beck-Huy
Illustrated by Shirley Moore Miller

Preface

It is an honor to write a preface for this book that explains the teachings of CaoDai to children. CaoDai is a new religion that seeks to reconcile the different religions of the world and to make a place in the world for tolerance and diversity. It was born in Vietnam during the colonial period, when Eastern religions and philosophies first entered into serious conversation with Western religions and philosophies. I came to learn about CaoDai by visiting a temple in Pomona, California, where Hum and Hong Bui were worshipping, and they have taught me a lot over a period of many years. I deeply value their sincerity and commitment to their faith, and I know that they are very well suited to explain these beliefs to others.

I hope this book will make some aspects of CaoDai accessible to children. CaoDai is a religion with many different levels of practice, and it is open to many different traditions. But it is based on certain moral and ethical principles and a shared understanding of the pathways to being united with God.

Every family wants to find a way to make their beliefs intelligible to children so that people of all ages can work together and share experiences. A book like this one provides an introduction to the most basic values but also suggests that there are areas that may require greater study or self-cultivation. People can choose to make a commitment to their religion at any age, but they still need some guidance to understand what they are committing themselves to doing. Relatively few materials about CaoDai are available in English, so this book makes a major contribution to understanding this new religion. It will be appreciated by both Vietnamese families whose children are mainly English speaking and non-Vietnamese people interested in discovering the basic principles of CaoDai.

As a student and researcher who has been learning about CaoDai for a number of years, I am very grateful to Hum and Hong Bui for the guidance they have given me, and I think this book will offer guidance to a new generation of people interested in CaoDai and seeking to learn its most basic principles.

Janet Hoskins
Professor of Anthropology, University of Southern California

Foreword

The diversity of religions brings about an array of uncertainties and mistrust between people of different traditions. CaoDai propounds the goal to unite religions in harmony and peace and to solve all human conflicts. It conceives that all humans are brothers and sisters from the same Father God. Each and every member of the human race has God's spirit inside, and with cultivation this spirit will be reunited with its noble origin.

This small book tries to provide an accessible account of the mission and practice of CaoDai, a faith of unity. Our profound, sincere wish is to see all people of the world living together as brothers and sisters under the same divine roof, as part of the family of God, and in peace inside and outside.

We want to express our sincere appreciation to all our children, grandchildren, and friends for their constant encouragement and invaluable assistance in the preparation of this book.

Hum D. Bui, MD
Hong D. Bui, MD

CaoDai: A Faith of Unity
A Parent and Child Book

God CaoDai

CaoDai (k_ d_) is a Vietnamese word that means "high tower, the place where God reigns." It is used as the name of God.

God is called by different names, such as Jehovah, Christ, Allah, Brahma, the nothingness, the Tao, Ahura Mazda, and Tai Chi.

God uses the name CaoDai to found a novel faith that has the mission to bring all religions together in harmony.

For CaoDai, we are all brothers and sisters.

We all come from one same God.

God CaoDai is present in all of us and in everything in the world.

Creation of the Universe

God created the universe.
The universe consists of the sun, the moon, the stars, and the planets.
One of the planets is Earth.
On Earth, there are minerals, plants, animals, and human beings.

God Commands the Universe

We cannot see God.
But we can feel God through all God's creations.
God commands everything in the universe: We can see the sun, moon, stars,
and planets; The sun shines during the day;
The moon shines at night;
The four seasons, spring, summer, autumn, and winter, continuously take
their turns.

The Earth

We can see the earth with its valleys, mountains, rivers, and forests.
We can see the plants bearing flowers and fruits.
We can see animals with their beautiful offspring, such as cubs and pups.
We can see human beings with beautiful children around.

We can feel God CaoDai inside ourselves. When we do good things to others either our parents, friends, or animals, we feel good. This is the feeling of God within ourselves.

God creates everything from His Great Sacred Energy and is therefore present in everything around us in the universe.

God's Teachings

The supreme being, CaoDai, teaches that God is in human beings, and human beings may become connected with God.

God is the Great Sacred Energy. Everything else has a little sacred energy and is part of the Great Sacred Energy. On the physical plane, scientists have discovered that electrons and protons are the common components of everything in the universe.

We may not see God, but we can feel the energy of God inside ourselves.

God Is the Way

God is the Tao, the Dao, or the Way.
Everything in the universe follows the Way in order to evolve.
God makes the Tao visible at different times, in different areas, and under different names to guide people to live in peace and harmony.

Religions: The Many Ways of God

In the East, God founded Hinduism and Buddhism in India.
In Hinduism, God is called *Brahma*.
In Buddhism, God is called *the nothingness*.
With meditation, we can reach the status of nothingness, which is when we are no longer attached to any bad emotions. Then we can have peace in our hearts and be unified with God.
God founded Taoism and Confucianism in China.
God is called *the Tao* in Taoism and *Tai-Chi* in Confucianism.
Taoism teaches to live in harmony with nature.
Confucianism teaches the human way, how to fulfill duties as a human being.

In the West, God founded Zoroastrianism, Judaism, Christianity, and Islam.
In Zoroastrianism, God is called *Ahura Mazda.*
In Judaism, God is called *Yahweh* (the English rendering of YHWH).
In Christianity, God is called *God,* and His only son is *Jesus Christ.*
In Islam, God is called *Allah.*
Later, God founded many other religions and spiritual movements around the world, such as Baha'i, Theosophy, the Unity Church, and Unitarian Universalism.

Are People Different?
People's Conflict

Now people find that they have so many differences:
They have different customs.
They speak different languages.
They eat different kinds of food.
They dress in different kinds of clothes.
Their religions are different.
They must compete to get what they need to survive.
Therefore, they have conflicts and sometimes fight over religion.

How to Solve the Conflict

God founded CaoDai to bring people together in peace, to tell them that all religions are one,
that all religions have the same origin: God.
They are all good. They teach the same principles: love and justice.
They are all trying to make peace. Although we have different appearances and diverse
lifestyles, we have the same God or CaoDai inside of us. CaoDai teaches people to love one
another and stop fighting over religion.

Spiritism

Everyone has God inside.
People may hear God's words inside.
But not everyone can hear God's words.
A person who can hear God's words directly is called a spirit medium.
A spirit medium can write down or speak out loud the words that he or she hears.
A séance (or spiritism) is a session in which God's words are recorded by a spirit medium.

How Was CaoDai Founded?

CaoDai was founded by God through spiritism.
In 1920, Mr. Ngô Văn Chiêu from Vietnam received God's words when he was the governor of Phú Quốc Island.
God ordered him to give messages to all religions and to all human beings that all religions are one and there is no difference between people; all of them have religious beliefs that should be respected.
People are just brothers and sisters of the same God family.
God taught Mr. Ngô Văn Chiêu meditation, a technique of calming down the mind in order to be connected with God and to feel God inside.

God's Words Were Also Heard in Saigon

In 1925, Mr. Cao Quỳnh Cư, Mr. Cao Hoài Sang, and Mr. Phạm Công Tắc also received God's words in Saigon, Vietnam, through séances with table tipping. God instructed them to look for Mr. Ngô Văn Chiêu and then to start the CaoDai faith together.

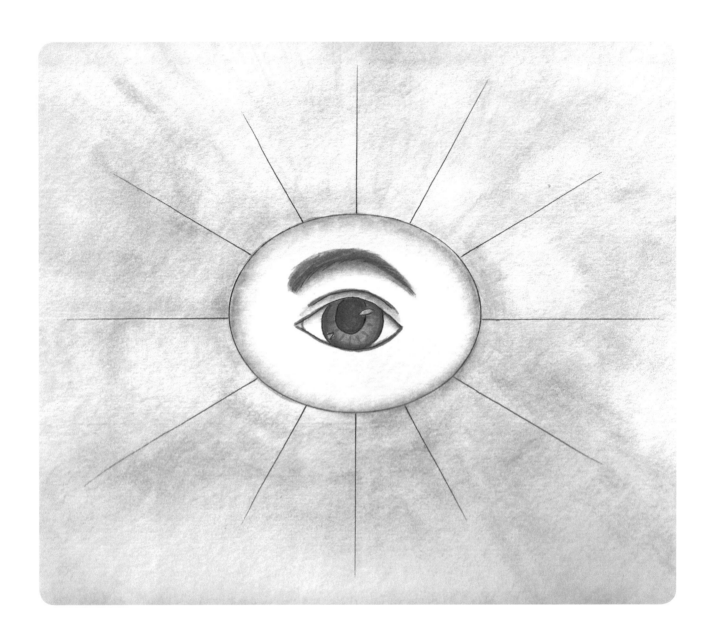

The Eye of God

God instructed them to use the all-seeing eye, the eye of God, as a symbol of the new faith because the all-seeing eye represents God, who is the spirit of the universe.

The Third Eye Center

In the human body, the all-seeing eye of God is believed to be at the third eye center. The third eye center is located inside the brain in the space between the two physical eyes.
With meditation, we concentrate on the third eye center and may reach a connection with God.

God's Principle

God taught human beings love and justice so they could live in peace and harmony.
"Love" is true love without conditions:
I love you because I love you, not because I want you to do something for me in return.
Justice is "Do not do to others what you don't want others to do to you," or "Don't harm others if you don't want others to harm you," or
"Do to others good things that you want others to do to you."
Always treat other people the way you want to be treated.

What Is True Love?

I love my mommy and my daddy.
I love a baby animal.

If I find a lost child, I comfort and help him or her.

When I see a baby bird falling out of its nest, I rescue it and put it back into its nest.
I help a blind person cross the street.

What Is Justice?

I don't want others to hurt me, so I don't hurt others.
I don't want others to ruin my toys, so I don't ruin the toys of others.

The Truth

God CaoDai taught this: "I am your master, and you are My children; I am you, and you are Me."
That means every one of us has God inside and may become one with God.
Similarly, the Buddha taught this: "The Buddha is in your heart; your heart is the Buddha."
or
"I am the Buddha already enlightened; you are the Buddha to be enlightened."
Everyone may feel the Buddha inside.
Everyone may become a Buddha.

Jesus Christ taught this: "My Father and I are one."
"God is in Me, and I am in God."
God is the truth, the way, and the life.
God is the Way, or the Tao.

Five Ways of the Tao

There are five ways of the Tao. They are all good and may be practiced singly or together.

The first way, or the human way, teaches people how to fulfill the duties of a human being.

For example, we must love our parents and follow our parents' guidance. When parents are old, children have to help their parents live happily.

We have to love our siblings, friends, and one another.

We have to love our neighbors and all other people and cooperate with them to live in peace and harmony in the community—regardless of their religious backgrounds, whether Buddhist, Hindu, Jew, Christian, Muslim, Confucian, Taoist, and so on.

In summary, we must be kind and loving to one another to be good human beings.

The second way is the way of heroes or angels.
We must open our hearts to serve greater groups in the community, to serve
the country as well as other human beings in the world.
In fulfilling this duty, a person is considered to be a real hero or an angel.
Mahatma Gandhi may be considered a hero or an angel.

The third way is the way of saints.
This way is represented by Moses, Jesus Christ, and Muhammad.
One may sacrifice oneself to serve humanity like Jesus did on the cross.
A recent example is Mother Teresa.
Mother Teresa served people with love and sacrifice until she died.
Mother Teresa is a saint.

The fourth way is the way of immortals.
In this way, a person is not involved with the suffering world.
He or she has no more material ambitions.
He or she cultivates and purifies himself or herself and may become an immortal.
This way is represented by Lao Tse, who cultivated himself and achieved an
everlasting happy life in the fairyland.

The fifth way is the way of Buddhas, where a person has no attachment with common life. Everything in the world is seen as temporary. It will decay and become dust, and therefore is considered as nothing.

When a person's mind and soul reach the status of nothingness, he or she will not suffer anymore. This way may liberate people from suffering.

This way is represented by the Buddha, who was enlightened by meditation and found ways to help humanity escape from worldly suffering and have peace inside.

CaoDai Worshipping

We worship God in front of the altar at home.
We worship at our convenient time—either at 6:00 a.m., at noon, at 6:00
p.m., or at midnight.
To worship God means to sincerely submit all of our body, mind, and soul to God.
Each one of us can directly communicate with God in prayer and meditation.

The Altar

The altar is the place where we submit ourselves sincerely to God.
On the altar is an all-seeing eye, the symbol of God, or the spirit of the
universe, who oversees everything in the universe and indeed understands
and knows every man, woman, and child.
We may also meditate in front of the altar.

The Five Precepts

Following the five precepts is a way to practice love and justice.
The five precepts are: 1. Do not kill; 2. Do not steal; 3. Do not commit adultery (to be unfaithful to one's family); 4. Do not get drunk or high; and 5. Do not lie or sin with words.

1. Do Not Kill

Do not kill people. Do not kill animals. Animals have lives and families just like us. A mother dog loves and takes care of her baby pups, and a mother cow loves and takes care of her baby calf. Do not kill them. Do not kill other animals either.
Do not kill people.
Not eating meat (being vegetarian) is a way to manifest the love of life.

2. Do Not Steal

You own things that belong to yourself. So do others.
We may share our things with others, and others may share their things with us.
But we cannot take things from others without permission.

3. Do Not Commit Adultery

Do not break the love and happiness of your family or others' families.

4. Do Not Get Drunk or High

Being drunk or intoxicated by drugs makes people confused.
They may get into accidents that may harm or kill others.

5. Do Not Lie or Sin with Words

Lying may cause lots of trouble to others. Lying may cause others to lose trust in us.

Practicing CaoDai

To practice CaoDai is to recognize and respect all religions because they are all one, coming from the same origin—God—and having the same ethics based on love and justice. To practice CaoDai is to follow the precepts, to serve others with love and justice, and to fulfill duties toward family, neighbors, communities, country, and humanity. We may pray and/ or meditate daily. Practicing CaoDai will bring us peace both inside and externally with all other people. In practicing CaoDai, we may still retain the identity of our religion (as a Jewish CaoDaist, Buddhist CaoDaist, Christian CaoDaist, etc.).

Each one of us can directly communicate with God in prayer and meditation.

God In Our Hearts

When we empty out emotions such as hatred, jealousy, sadness, anger, worry, greed, and confusion, we have a place in our hearts for God to come in. When we meditate, we sit calmly and breathe slowly. This is good for our health. When we do not think about anything except love, love to all in nature, then God comes to our hearts.

Union with God

When we are in union with God, we feel extremely happy.

References

CaoDai is the name of God.
God uses the name CaoDai to found a novel faith, which has the mission to bring all religions together in harmony.

CaoDai is the abbreviation of Cao Đài Tiên Ông Đại Bồ Tát Ma Ha Tát, the full symbolic name of God. Cao Đài means the Supreme Palace where God reigns and is a Confucian term representing God. Tiên Ông is the lowest rank in Taoism. Đại Bồ Tát Ma Ha Tát is the lowest rank in Buddhism. Together, Cao Đài Tiên Ông Đại Bồ Tát Ma Ha Tát, the full symbolic name of God, represents not only the unification of the three main religions but also the humility of God, who comes to humanity as the lowest rank in religions. (Bui, *CaoDaism, A Novel Religion,* 1992, p. 33)

For CaoDai, we are all brothers and sisters. We all come from one same God. God CaoDai is present in all of us and in everything in the world.

"You do not need to have the same name to be in the same family.
By following the same Way, you all have the same father.
In this lifespan of one hundred years, remember to serve humanity,
and try your best to teach each other concordance"
(*Collection of Selected Holy Messages,* 1972, p. 8).

God created the universe.
In the universe, there are the sun, moon, stars, and planets.

"Before the creation of the heavens and the universe, the cosmic ether was still, quiet, and void; and at the same time a kind of primordial chaos, indistinct and shadowy with mixtures of density (which we call "the Tao" or pre-creation ether). In this cosmic ether appeared a great source of Divine Light called "Thái Cực" (Monad) or the Supreme Being. The Monad then divided itself into Yin and Yang, the two opposite logos: "*Âm* Quang" (Yin Darkness) and "Dương Quang" (Yang Energy). Yin is heavy, dark, cold, dense, passive, and inactive, while Yang is clear, bright, warm, pure, positive, and active … Yin and Yang interacted with each other to form heavens and universes, with Yang being the origin of the invisible, spiritual aspect, and Yin being the mother of all visible, physical manifestations"
(*Đại Thừa Chơn Giáo, The True Teachings of the Great Wheel,* 1936, p. 216).

One of the planets is Earth.
On Earth, there are materials, plants, animals, and human beings.

"After creating the universe, I divided My spirit and with it made all creatures, plants, and materials. Everything in this universe comes from My spirit and therefore has a life. Where there is life, there is Myself, even in materials and plants. I am each of you, and you are Me"
(*Thánh Ngôn Hiệp Tuyển, Collection of Selected Holy Messages,* 1972, p. 170).

We cannot see God.
But we can feel God through all God's creations.
God commands everything in the universe. We can see the sun, moon, stars, and planets.
The sun shines during the day.
The moon shines at night.
The four seasons, spring, summer, autumn, and winter, continuously take their turns.

"Does Heaven ever speak?
The four seasons come and go,
And all creatures thrive and grow.
Does Heaven ever speak?"
(Confucius Analects)

The supreme being, CaoDai, teaches that God is in human beings, and human beings may become God.

"With only My spirit, I have created Buddhas, Immortals, Saints, Angels, and all human beings in this universe. Therefore, I am you, and you are Me"
(*Thánh Ngôn Hiệp Tuyển, Collection of Selected Holy Messages,* 1972, p. 27).

God is the Great Sacred Energy.
Everything else has a little sacred energy and is part of the Great Sacred Energy.

"On earth, you are a sacred light,
And are part of My Sacred Light.
You already have the key,
To go anywhere - to earth or to heaven"
(*Thánh Giáo Sưu Tập, Collection of Holy Messages,* 1966-67, p. 36).

"I and My Father are One"
(John 10:30)

God or the Supreme Being is the Tao, the Dao, or the Way.
Everything in the universe follows the Way in order to evolve.

"There was something nebulous, existing before the heaven and earth, silent, empty, standing alone, altering not, moving cyclically without being exhausted, and which may be called the mother of all under heaven. I do not know its name; call it Tao"
(*Tao Te Ching,* 25).

God creates the Tao at different times, in different areas, and under different names to guide people to live in peace and harmony. In the East, God founded Hinduism and Buddhism in India.
In Hinduism, God is called *Brahma.*

In Buddhism, God is called *the nothingness.*
God founded Taoism and Confucianism in China.
God is called *the Tao* in Taoism and *Tai-Chi* in Confucianism.
In the West, God founded Zoroastrianism, Judaism, Christianity, and Islam.
In Zoroastrianism, God is called *Ahura Mazda.*
In Judaism, God is called *Yahweh.*
In Christianity, God is called *God,* and His only son is *Jesus Christ.*
In Islam, God is called *Allah.*
Now people find that they have so many differences in all aspects of their lives.
They have different customs.
They speak different languages.
They eat different kinds of food.
They dress in different kinds of clothes.
Their religions are different.
They must compete to get what they need to survive.
Therefore, they have conflicts and sometimes fight over religion.
God founded CaoDai to bring people together in peace, to tell them that all religions are one, that all religions have the same origin, God. All religions teach the same principles: love and justice.
Although we have different appearances and diverse lifestyles, we have the same God or CaoDai inside of us.

"Formerly, people lacked transportation and therefore did not know each other, I then founded at different epochs and in different areas, five branches of the Great Way: The way of humanity, the way of angels and heroes, the way of Saints, the way of Immortals, and the way of Buddhas, each based on the customs of the race. In present days, transportation has been improved, and people have come to know each other better. But people do not always live in harmony because of the very multiplicity of those religions. That is why I have decided to unite all those religions into one to bring them to the primordial unity"
(*Thánh Ngôn Hiệp Tuyển, Collection of Selected Holy Messages,* 1972, p. 16).

Everyone has God inside.
People may hear God's words inside.
But not everyone can hear God's words.
A person who can hear God's words directly is called a spirit medium.
A spirit medium can write down or speak out loud the words that he or she hears.
A séance is a session in which God's words are recorded by a spirit medium.

"In spiritism, the medium must meditate deeply so that his spirit will then be able to come to Me, listen to My instructions, and have his body to write down the messages. What is a spirit? The spirit is your second body. It is very difficult for the spirit of a human being to transcend the physical body. The spirits of Saints, Immortals, and Buddhas are very marvelous and immortal. The spirit of an enlightened person may transcend the body and even travel the universe. Only the spirit may approach Me. When the basket with beak is used in spiritism, if

the person is unconscious, the spirit may then leave the physical body, hear My instructions, and have the body transcribe the messages"
(*Thánh Ngôn Hiệp Tuyển, Collection of Selected Holy Messages,* 1972, p. 6).

God instructed them to use the all-seeing eye, the eye of God, as a symbol of the new faith because the all-seeing eye represents God.

"The heart manifests at the eye
Presiding everything are two sources of light (Yin and Yang);
Light is spirit;
Spirit is God"
(*Thánh Ngôn Hiệp Tuyển, Collection of Selected Holy Messages,* 1972, p. 11).

Justice is "Do not do to others what you don't want others to do to you," or "Do to others good things that you want others to do to you."

"Do not do to others what you don't want them to do to you"
(Confucius Analects 15:23).
"Do unto others as you would have them do unto you."
(Matthew 7:12).

When we empty out emotions such as hatred, jealousy, sadness, anger, worry, greed, confusion, we have a place in our hearts for God to come in.
When we meditate, we sit calmly and breathe slowly.
When we do not think about anything except love, love to all in nature, then God comes to our hearts.

"When there is sincerity in the heart, the physical body would be secure. If the heart is not controlled, there would be danger. Self-cultivation is to calm down the heart. Then, there would be peace in the heart and in life"
(*Thánh Giáo Sưu Tập, Collection of Holy Messages*).

Contact

For further inquiries or comments, please contact CAODAI OVERSEAS, 808 W. Vermont Avenue, Anaheim, CA 92805, USA, or email hongbui24568@gmail.com, or humbui@caodai.org. Or visit the website www.caodai.org.

Hum D. Bui, MD, was born to a CaoDai family, and Hong D. Bui, MD, was born to a Buddhist family in Vietnam. They are now under the same CaoDai roof. Husband and wife, they came to the United States in 1975 and began sharing the religious unity and oneness of CaoDai teachings with the Western world. Together, they have participated in interfaith activities in Rome; Mt. Hiei, Japan; Cape Town, South Africa; Barcelona, Spain; Montreal, Canada; Seoul, South Korea; and the United States. They continue translating CaoDai teachings into English and maintain a CaoDai website, www.caodai.org.

Ngasha Beck-Huy is a born intuitive and has been a practitioner of the esoteric arts since age eleven. In 1993 she received a vision of the Divine Eye and was led to make contact with the CaoDai community under the guidance of the spirit of Victor Hugo; she presently fulfills her dharmic obligations as editor of the English versions of CaoDai writings and messages.

Other books by Hum D. Bui and Hong D. Bui:

Thượng Đế Đã *Giáng Trần—God Has Come,* 1990 (Chân Tâm)
Pháp Chánh Truyền—The Religious Constitution of CaoDaism, 1992 (translation) (Chân Tâm)
CaoDaism, A Novel Religion, 1992 (Chân Tâm)
CaoDai, Faith of Unity, 2000 (Emerald Wave)
Guide to CaoDai Spiritual Celebration, 2006 (Chân Tâm)
Collection of Selected Holy Messages (Parts I and II). Translation. E-book at www.scribd. com/doc/23193583/Collection-of-Cao-Dai-Holy-Messages-17261598

About the Author
Hum D. Bui, MD, and his wife Hong have four children. Both doctors, Hum and Hong are working at a free clinic and spend time in various interfaith activities. Hum is also the author of several other CaoDai works.

About the Book
CaoDai: A Faith of Unity discusses the oneness between God, human beings, and the universe, including religions. Religions share the same divine origin and ethics based on love and justice, and they are just different manifestations of one truth. If human beings realize the oneness between God, human beings, and religions, the world may achieve harmony.

"CaoDai is a new religion that seeks to reconcile the different religions of the world and make a place in the world for tolerance and diversity."
Janet Hoskins
Professor of Anthropology, University of Southern California

"This book is not only a simple explanation of the CaoDai faith appropriate for children and families but also a simple explanation of many of the mysteries around religions that any interfaith seeker could find useful. It is a blessing to see an interfaith understanding come from a religion of the East that includes Western traditions. The interfaith vision of the CaoDai faith can serve as a model for all of us and may bring us back to the interfaith visions of the founders of many religious traditions of the world."
Reverend Jan Chase
Minister, Unity Church of Pomona

Printed in the United States
By Bookmasters